# Little RIDDLERS

## Northamptonshire

Edited By Jenni Harrison

First published in Great Britain in 2018 by:

 Young**Writers**

Young Writers
Remus House
Coltsfoot Drive
Peterborough
PE2 9BF
Telephone: 01733 890066
Website: www.youngwriters.co.uk

# FOREWORD

Dear Reader,

Are you ready to get your thinking caps on to puzzle your way through this wonderful collection?

Young Writers' Little Riddlers competition set out to encourage young writers to create their own riddles. Their answers could be whatever or whoever their imaginations desired; from people to places, animals to objects, food to seasons. Riddles are a great way to further the children's use of poetic expression, including onomatopoeia and similes, as well as encourage them to 'think outside the box' by providing clues without giving the answer away immediately.

All of us here at Young Writers believe in the importance of inspiring young children to produce creative writing, including poetry, and we feel that seeing their own riddles in print will keep that creative spirit burning brightly and proudly.

We hope you enjoy riddling your way through this book as much as we enjoyed reading all the entries.

# CONTENTS

Cameron W (7) 59
Hargun Singh (7) 60

## Mears Ashby CE Primary School, Mears Ashby

Jackson Cebula (7) 61
Max Perrett-King (7) 62
Elijah Borbor (7) 63
Jesse Leah (6) 64
Imogen Xanthe Walker (5) 65
Alba McNaught (6) 66
Frankie Thomas Hewer (7) 67
Dawson Goodrick (7) 68
Thomas Admans (7) 69
Archie William Charles 70
Worthington (6)
Amelia Difonzo-Yamoah (5) 71
Henry Crabtree (5) 72
Tejay Rushton (6) 73
Jessica Cooling (6) 74

## Pitsford School, Pitsford

Jemima Poppy Wilmer (7) 75
Hadi Choudary (7) 76
Henry Morriss (6) 77
Noah Hulme (7) 78
Henry Schwartz-Jones (5) 79
Erin Amirak (6) 80
Ava Thompson (5) 81
Hannah Muriva (5) 82
Isla McNally (6) 83

## St Luke's CE Primary School, Duston

Leyton Considine (7) 84
Shanice Makoni (6) 85
Rylee Star Sawyer (6) 86
Sienna Tomes (7) 87
Alice Olivia Abdy (6) 88
Lily Grace Birch (6) 89
Caleb Tew (6) 90

Bella Maranzano (7) 91
Sasha Chikandwa (6) 92
Lucy-Anne Hever (6) 93
Lamont Tristan M (6) 94
Sophia Mabuto (7) 95
Maegan Nicole Anderton (6) 96
Isla Eve Redding (7) 97
Harry Timothy Roberts (5) 98
Zack Linnane (7) 99
Ryan Woodfield (6) 100
Luke Try (6) 101
Evie Clark (6) 102
Anelise Otilia Stanciu (7) 103
Lily-Mae Richards (6) 104
Lily Sue Frost (6) 105
Jessie Ivy Rose Lodge (6) 106
Jenson Falkner (6) 107
Katarina Berberic (6) 108
Amelia-Rose Richardson (5) 109
Annabelle Brown (6) 110
Daniel Rees (6) 111
Joy Bonsu (7) 112
Alice Shepherd (7) 113
Archie Ronald Britten (6) 114
Harrison Lovekin (7) 115
Fleur Boobyer (5) 116
Grace Lauren Louise Dolman (6) 117
Paige Hayward (5) 118
Charlie Littlewood (6) 119
Lewis Smith (6) 120
Abbie Renda (6) 121
Paige McDonnell (6) 122
Rishab Jain (5) 123
Tony Singh (6) 124
Lewis Pearson (6) 125
Iulia Duta (6) 126
Zachary Morley (6) 127
Andrei Marinescu (6) 128
Jessica Redzaj (5) 129
Arthur Haslam (5) 130
Callum Muldoon (5) 131
Ashden Copeland (5) 132
Emily Cripps (6) 133

| | |
|---|---|
| Maksymilian Wojciechowski (7) | 134 |
| Noah Hyliands (5) | 135 |
| Micah Siziba (5) | 136 |
| Sebastian Jeffreys (7) | 137 |
| Lewis Liu (7) | 138 |
| Elizabeth Cook (5) | 139 |
| Maisie Turner (7) | 140 |
| Ella May Vine (6) | 141 |
| Sam Connolly-Green (6) | 142 |
| Krystian Redel (7) | 143 |
| Logan Hayes (7) | 144 |
| Aaron Baker (5) | 145 |
| Liliko Dhesi (6) | 146 |
| Summer Jade Anderton (5) | 147 |
| Ameena Abimbola Adekoya (7) | 148 |
| Elliot King (5) | 149 |
| Ava-Mae Lowry (5) | 150 |
| Grayson Hughes (5) | 151 |
| Zakaria Kunhalil (6) | 152 |
| Imogen Castle (6) | 153 |
| Oscar Gibbins (6) | 154 |
| Aurelia Taylor (4) | 155 |
| Ruben Holt (6) | 156 |
| Scarlett Lily-May Craven (5) | 157 |
| Harley Nichols (6) | 158 |
| Leo V (6) | 159 |
| George Hamer (5) | 160 |
| Vinnie Ogden (5) | 161 |
| Filip Chomicki (6) | 162 |
| Poppy Kenton (5) | 163 |
| Noah Morris (7) | 164 |
| Faith Brothers (7) | 165 |
| Erioluwa Tioluwa Nathan Oyetunde (5) | 166 |
| Isioma Divine Ohaeli (4) | 167 |

## Upton Meadows Primary School, Upton

| | |
|---|---|
| Julia Wozniak (6) | 168 |

# THE POEMS

# Lewis' Riddle

I am full of balls.
I am fun.
I am big.
I have colourful balls.
I am for playing in.
I am for children.
What am I?

Answer: A ball pit.

## Lewis Bourn (9)
Billing Brook School, Lumbertubs

# Lorrie's Riddle

I am full of balls.
I am square shaped.
I have blue walls.
I have colourful balls.
I am fun to play in.
What am I?

Answer: A ball pit.

## Lorrie Bateman (8)
Billing Brook School, Lumbertubs

# Tori's Riddle

I have a long neck.
I have a long tail.
I am spotty.
I have hooves.
I have short fur.
What am I?

Answer: A giraffe.

## Tori Humphreys (7)
Billing Brook School, Lumbertubs

# Muhammed's Riddle

I have colourful balls.
I am fun.
I am squishy.
I am for playing.
I am soft.
What am I?

*Answer: A ball pit.*

## Muhammed Ahmed (8)
Billing Brook School, Lumbertubs

# Georgia's Riddle

I am pretty.
I smell like nectar.
Bees go in me.
Some are pink.
Some are blue.
What am I?

Answer: Flowers.

## Georgia O'Callaghan (9)
Billing Brook School, Lumbertubs

# Bradley's Riddle

I have hooves.
I am spotty.
I am tall.
I am brown.
I have a long neck.
What am I?

Answer: A giraffe.

## Bradley Mushauripo (9)
Billing Brook School, Lumbertubs

# Kye's Riddkle

I am brown.
I am funny.
I have black spots.
I have a tail.
I am big.
Who am I?

Answer: Scooby Doo.

## Kye Smith (8)
Billing Brook School, Lumbertubs

# Brain Eaters

I'm in horror films
I'll eat your brain
We come out of graves at night
You kill us with a cricket bat
Our eyes come out of our green, rotten
faces
We drag our feet
What am I?

Answer: A zombie.

## Sidney Middleditch (7)
Eastfield Academy, Northampton

# What Could I Be?

I am big, I am small.
I swing from trees and climb them all.
I like bananas, I eat them all.
Most important I am the cutest of them all.
What am I?

Answer: A monkey.

## Charley Jak Ashton-Ford (7)
Eastfield Academy, Northampton

# Summer Fruits

I'm very juicy and tasty.
You can find me in farms, fields and even supermarkets.
I come in different colours.
I've got seeds.
I've got a stem, try not to eat it.
If you're hot in the summer it's very good to eat me.
What am I?

Answer: A strawberry.

## Lauren Dunton (11)

Friars Academy, Wellingborough

# Green Blocks

I am not a living thing.
You can have fun with me.
You can build things with blocks.
Online is a great way to deal with me.
You will enjoy killing the monsters and mining for bricks.
Playing me with a friend is best.
What am I?

Answer: Minecraft.

## Kally Smith (11)

Friars Academy, Wellingborough

# Seasons Greetings

I appear from December to February.
You can make a snowman when I am here.
You need to wrap up warm when I am here.
You see my snow.
Christmas Day happens when I am here.
Leaves fall down when I am here.
What am I?

Answer: Winter.

## Callum Sleafer (12)
Friars Academy, Wellingborough

# Science Teachers Like Me

I need gas to work.
I have a yellow and orange flame.
I have two types of flames.
I get really hot.
If you touch me you will get hurt.
You can find me in the science lab.
What am I?

Answer: A Bunsen burner.

## Paul Green (11)
Friars Academy, Wellingborough

# Midnight

I only appear on the darkest midnight,
With the moon as full as it can be.
My howl would be heard for miles,
While I roam the forest hunting prey.
My tail is as fluffy as can be.
What am I?

Answer: A werewolf.

## Dylan White (11)
Friars Academy, Wellingborough

# Jack's Riddle

I come in different sizes.
I have a long tail.
I have sharp claws.
I used to rule the land.
I lived in different time periods.
I lived between 65 to 240 million years ago.
What am I?

Answer: A dinosaur.

## Jack Goss (11)
Friars Academy, Wellingborough

# Noise

There are all types of me.
Hear me through your iPod headphones.
I make you boogie and sing
And give you good feelings.
Little Mix makes lots of me.
I can really calm you down.
What am I?

Answer: Music

## Kimberley Marie Letts (11)

Friars Academy, Wellingborough

# A Box Full Of Games

I can be black or white.
People call me a box but I'm not really a box.
I have a controller.
I'm good to play games on.
The TV is my friend.
I have an X on me.
What am I?

Answer: An Xbox.

## Kyle Herd (12)
Friars Academy, Wellingborough

# After A Beef Dinner

I can be made with cheese
Or with ice cream.
Sometimes I have sprinkles.
You can take me on a picnic.
Icing makes me yummy.
The chocolate on me can melt.
What am I?.

Answer: A cake.

## Jamie Summers (11)
Friars Academy, Wellingborough

# What Am I?

I have small eyes because I don't need them.
I don't have legs.
I like swimming in the water.
I have blue flippers.
I have a horn to crack foes.
I eat shrimp and squid.
I have blubber.
I live in the Arctic.
What am I?

Answer: A narwhal.

## Sonia Frances Kornacka (7)
Kings Heath Primary Academy, Kings Heath

# What Am I?

I can smash ice.
I have a horn.
I am a type of whale.
I am very big.
I have fins to swim in the cold, icy sea.
I have blubber to keep warm.
I eat squid and shrimp.
What am I?

Answer: A narwhal.

## Riley Loader (6)
Kings Heath Primary Academy, Kings Heath

# What Am I?

I have two tusks.
I have a body full of blubber.
I have three whiskers on each side of my face.
I have black eyes.
I swim.
I do not have legs.
I live on ice.
What am I?

Answer: A walrus.

## Jack Sweeney (6)
Kings Heath Primary Academy, Kings Heath

# What Am I?

I like to run in the snow and pull sledges.
I have four legs.
I have black and white fur.
I can be kept as a pet.
I eat meat and fish.
I live in the Arctic.
What am I?

Answer: A husky.

## Milana Cinnell (6)
Kings Heath Primary Academy, Kings Heath

# What Am I?

I have four legs.
I have white fur.
I have sharp claws.
I like to live in snow.
I have thick blubber.
I have sharp teeth.
I eat fish and seals.
What am I?

Answer: A polar bear.

## Vivienne Pawlak (6)
Kings Heath Primary Academy, Kings Heath

# What Am I?

I can run in the snow.
I have dark blue and white fur.
I can pull sledges.
I have sharp claws.
I live in North Europe.
I have four legs.
I eat fish.
What am I?

Answer: A husky.

## Darja Maksunova (6)
Kings Heath Primary Academy, Kings Heath

# What Am I?

I have two legs.
I have different types of skin so I am not a chicken.
I am sometimes owned by pirates
Or people who are not pirates.
I have a black beak.
What am I?

Answer: A parrot.

## Aiden Marszalek (7)
Kings Heath Primary Academy, Kings Heath

# What Am I?

I have teeth so I am not a seal.
I have grey skin so I'm not a reindeer.
I like eating fish and salmon.
I swim in water through the cracked ice.
What am I?

Answer: A narwhal.

## Dionis Vargo (7)
Kings Heath Primary Academy, Kings Heath

# What Am I?

I have white fur.
I can blend into the snow.
I am not a polar bear.
I have a bushy tail.
When I go to sleep I cover my body with my tail.
What am I?

Answer: An Arctic fox.

## Orianne Hamilton (6)
Kings Heath Primary Academy, Kings Heath

# What Am I?

I can swim in the freezing sea.
I have four flippers, I don't run.
I eat fish.
I have no fur.
I can swim in the cold sea.
I am grey.
What am I?

Answer: A walrus.

## Kira Somogyi-Berta (6)
Kings Heath Primary Academy, Kings Heath

# What Am I?

I am colossal.
I am rotten and petrifying.
I am like a dangerous tornado.
I have sharp claws and huge teeth.
I am fluffy and smooth.
What am I?

Answer: A dragon.

## Joshua Ibbeson (6)
Kings Heath Primary Academy, Kings Heath

# What Am I?

I like to break ice.
I have a sharp horn.
I swim in the sea.
I have blubber.
I have no feet.
I eat shrimp and squid.
What am I?

Answer: A narwhal.

## Jude Underwood (6)

Kings Heath Primary Academy, Kings Heath

# What Am I?

I am ferocious.
I am vile and fluffy.
I am like a pterodactyl.
I am as hot as fire and ferocious.
I am petrifying.
What am I?

Answer: A dragon.

## Lilian Hall (5)
Kings Heath Primary Academy, Kings Heath

# What Am I?

I'm white and I hunt in the snow.
I have four legs.
I can run fast.
I live in the cold.
I eat fish.
What am I?

Answer: An Arctic fox.

## Sawson Ali (6)

Kings Heath Primary Academy, Kings Heath

# What Am I?

I am scaly and ginormous.
I am large.
I am huge.
I am scary.
I am like a hot fire.
I am ferocious.
What am I?

Answer: A dragon.

**Imran Ali (5)**
Kings Heath Primary Academy, Kings Heath

# What Am I?

I am strong.
I am tough.
I am like a giant crocodile.
I am as scary as a baddy.
I am perilous.
What am I?

Answer: A dragon.

## Lilly Tipping (6)
Kings Heath Primary Academy, Kings Heath

# What Am I?

I am sapphire.
I am camouflaged and kind.
I am like a scary storm.
I am terrifying like a bee.
What am I?

Answer: A dragon.

## Lola Etheridge (5)
Kings Heath Primary Academy, Kings Heath

# What Am I?

I have a big horn to fight.
I swim in the cold sea.
I eat squid and shrimp.
I have flippers.
What am I?

Answer: A narwhal.

## Abdullaahi Aadan (6)
Kings Heath Primary Academy, Kings Heath

# What Am I?

I have sharp teeth.
I have thick, white fur.
I have sharp claws.
I have cute baby cubs.
What am I?

Answer: A polar bear.

**Emily Adams (6)**
Kings Heath Primary Academy, Kings Heath

# What Am I?

I am soft.
I am huge and vile.
I am like a flying horse.
I have sharp claws.
What am I?

Answer: A dragon.

## Makayla Balogun (5)
Kings Heath Primary Academy, Kings Heath

# What Am I?

I am colossal.
I am kind.
I am petrifying.
I am smooth.
I am spiky.
What am I?

Answer: A dragon.

## Ahmed Toyi (5)
Kings Heath Primary Academy, Kings Heath

# What Am I?

I have a horn.
I swim in the sea.
I have a fin.
I eat squid and swim.
What am I?

Answer: A walrus.

## Haitham Ahmed (7)
Kings Heath Primary Academy, Kings Heath

# What Am I?

I am a knight's enemy.
I am dark.
I am spiky.
I am ferocious.
What am I?

Answer: A dragon.

## Sebby Holley (5)
Kings Heath Primary Academy, Kings Heath

# What Am I?

I am scaly and black.
I am vicious and dangerous.
I am fiery and dark.
What am I?

*Answer: A dragon.*

## Maja Kaczmarczyk (5)
Kings Heath Primary Academy, Kings Heath

# What Am I?

I am scaly.
I am massive and petrifying.
I am like a ferocious lion.
What am I?

Answer: A dragon.

## Ryder Phoebe Hurding (5)

Kings Heath Primary Academy, Kings Heath

# What Am I?

I am massive.
I am camouflaged and fluffy.
I am like a hot volcano.
What am I?

*Answer: A dragon.*

## Callum Collyer (5)
Kings Heath Primary Academy, Kings Heath

# What Am I?

I am bonkers.
I am like a dinosaur and a bear.
I am ferocious.
What am I?

Answer: A dragon.

## Ayesha Abdul-Alim (6)
Kings Heath Primary Academy, Kings Heath

# What Am I?

I am ruby-red.
I am dangerous and scary.
I am like a T-rex.
What am I?

Answer: A dragon.

## Muhammad Miah (6)
Kings Heath Primary Academy, Kings Heath

# What Am I?

I am scaly
I am intimidating.
I am like a snake.
What am I?

Answer: A dragon.

## Izzy Robinson (5)
Kings Heath Primary Academy, Kings Heath

# What Am I?

I am colossal.
I am scaly.
I am petrifying.
What am I?

*Answer: A dragon.*

## Jayleigh Spencer (5)
Kings Heath Primary Academy, Kings Heath

# What Am I?

I am scary.
I am scaly.
I am intimidating.
What am I?

Answer: A dragon.

## Lukasz Zalewski (5)

Kings Heath Primary Academy, Kings Heath

# What Am I?

I am ferocious.
I am scary.
I am furious.
What am I?

Answer: A dragon.

## Eloise Long (6)
Kings Heath Primary Academy, Kings Heath

# What Am I?

I am shark-like.
I am dark.
I am scary.
What am I?

Answer: A dragon.

## Kinga Krawczynska (5)
Kings Heath Primary Academy, Kings Heath

# What Am I?

I am scary.
I am fiery.
I am gigantic.
What am I?

Answer: A dragon.

## Joey Laws (5)
Kings Heath Primary Academy, Kings Heath

# What Am I?

I am dark.
I am scary.
I am lava.
What am I?

Answer: A dragon.

## Mildred Harry (6)
Kings Heath Primary Academy, Kings Heath

# Play Well

Sometimes I can be difficult to play with.
I come in many colours and sizes.
Boys and girls can build with me.
I am very old.
I have a land named after me,
I also have my own shops.
I hurt your feet when you step on me.
I used to be wood but now I'm plastic.
Build me strong, build me weak.
I have bits on top of me, you can build with me.
What am I?

Answer: A Lego brick.

## Ben Shimmin (7)
Lings Primary School, Lings

# My Speedy Transporter

I can be ridden in the park
If it's light or if it's dark.
I am low to the ground,
I can make a lot of sounds.
I can be a kid's dream,
Mine makes me beam.
I could win a great race,
With the wind in my face.
What am I?

Answer: A go-kart.

## Max Blewitt (7)
Lings Primary School, Lings

# Stripy Lady

I am a flying insect,
I make a buzzing sound,
I have two antennae, two eyes and two wings,
If you hurt my tail, I will sting,
My friends bring me lots of pollen,
My honey makes yummy honeycomb,
What am I?

Answer: A queen bee.

## Parina Pallavi Vaghela (6)
Lings Primary School, Lings

# What Am I?

I have a wet nose.
I have big pointy ears.
I don't have much of a tail.
I have four legs and love to play in the woods.
My favourite thing to do is cuddle.
What am I?

*Answer: A French bulldog.*

## Chloe Fox (6)
Lings Primary School, Lings

# Superheroes

I'm the light side.
A ninja in the shadows.
I always wear a bandana.
I'm fast and super strong.
I have got a small shell on my back.
What am I?

Answer: A ninja turtle.

## Jayden Abrokwah (7)
Lings Primary School, Lings

# Toy Story

I am a rectangle.
I have circles on top.
I am from Denmark.
You can stack me up.
I am made of plastic.
I have instructions.
What am I?

Answer: A Lego brick.

## Cameron W (7)
Lings Primary School, Lings

# Pride

I always roam around the world.
I never come to the Earth.
I awake in the night and sleep in the day.
Nights are dark without me.
What am I?

Answer: The moon.

## Hargun Singh (7)
Lings Primary School, Lings

# Sneaky Slitherer

I curl tightly and I squeeze the breath out of my unfortunate prey.
I slither gently across the ground like a snail.
I hang around on branches high up in the scalding sky.
I live in different places like Australia and New Zealand.
I'm small but beastly.
I don't have any beastly, sharp teeth.
I don't have any arms or legs.
What am I?

Answer: A snake.

## Jackson Cebula (7)
Mears Ashby CE Primary School, Mears Ashby

# Space

I zoom in space looking for planets to land on.
I whizz past planets I've landed on.
I keep an eye on where I'm going.
I look down on Earth, it's a beautiful sight.
I have a jet which gives me the power to whizz everywhere.
What am I?

Answer: A rocket.

## Max Perrett-King (7)
Mears Ashby CE Primary School, Mears Ashby

# Fast Runner

I am as skinny as a cat.
I am as fast as a car.
I can see things from a mile away.
I chase prey, catch prey, eat prey.
I jump as high as a rock.
I camouflage so my prey doesn't see me.
What am I?

Answer: A cheetah.

## Elijah Borbor (7)
Mears Ashby CE Primary School, Mears Ashby

# Long Stretchy Worm

I am as fat as a worm.
I can live up to two hundred years old.
I am dark.
I eat green, round leaves.
I am as long as a worm.
I travel really far.
I live everywhere.
What am I?

Answer: A centipede.

## Jesse Leah (6)
Mears Ashby CE Primary School, Mears Ashby

# Large Eyes

I am as long as a tree
And I've got a very long neck and large
eyes.
I am very dangerous and have sharp teeth.
I am dark colours and scary.
I am calm but be aware.
What am I?

Answer: A hammerhead shark.

## Imogen Xanthe Walker (5)
Mears Ashby CE Primary School, Mears Ashby

# Light

I'm like the sun.
I can see the sea.
I can feel the breeze.
I'm making a sandcastle.
Time to get squirted.
I can touch a flower.
*Splash-splash.*
What am I?

Answer: Summer.

## Alba McNaught (6)
Mears Ashby CE Primary School, Mears Ashby

# Slither Writher

I am as fast as a cheetah.
I can camouflage in the long, wet grass.
I am as mean as a crocodile.
My teeth are sharp like a knife.
I am a hunter in the jungle.
What am I?

Answer: A snake.

## Frankie Thomas Hewer (7)
Mears Ashby CE Primary School, Mears Ashby

# Horned Jumper

I am as stripy as a tiger.
My horns are as long as branches.
I run in a herd.
I have really skinny legs.
I can jump over a cactus.
What am I?

Answer: A gazelle.

## Dawson Goodrick (7)
Mears Ashby CE Primary School, Mears Ashby

# Black As Night

I am as big as a dragon.
I am over two thousand years old.
I live up in in the air.
People rarely step on me.
I light up the sky.
What am I?

Answer: The moon.

## Thomas Admans (7)
Mears Ashby CE Primary School, Mears Ashby

# On The Farm

I say *chug-chug-chug.*
I help to do the farming.
I feed the animals.
Whatever you do don't go near me.
What am I?

Answer: A tractor.

## Archie William Charles Worthington (6)

Mears Ashby CE Primary School, Mears Ashby

# Gold

I have a purple dress.
I have beautiful, long, golden hair.
I have the biggest castle ever.
I have a pink strap.
What am I?

Answer: A princess.

## Amelia Difonzo-Yamoah (5)
Mears Ashby CE Primary School, Mears Ashby

# The Beast

I am very scary.
I've got four legs.
I've got a mane.
I live in my cave.
I chase my prey.
What am I?

Answer: A lion.

## Henry Crabtree (5)
Mears Ashby CE Primary School, Mears Ashby

# Eight Fins

I have eight fins.
I can breathe underwater.
I have sharp teeth.
I gobble up fish.
What am I?

Answer: A bull shark.

## Tejay Rushton (6)
Mears Ashby CE Primary School, Mears Ashby

# Fluffy

I am as fluffy as a cloud.
I am as short as a cat.
I have long ears.
I bark very loud.
What am I?

Answer: A dog.

## Jessica Cooling (6)
Mears Ashby CE Primary School, Mears Ashby

# What Am I?

I am active at night.
There are about 200 different kinds of me.
I hunt insects and small mammals.
I have powerful talons.
I live in a parliament.
Sometimes I hunt fish.
What am I?

Answer: An owl.

**Jemima Poppy Wilmer (7)**
Pitsford School, Pitsford

# What Am I?

There are different kinds of me.
Some of us live on the ground.
Some of us live in the trees.
I have a curly tail.
I am not the same as an ape.
What am I?

Answer: A monkey.

## Hadi Choudary (7)
Pitsford School, Pitsford

# What Am I?

I am so smart for two years old.
I slurp water.
I can sense time.
I can hear very well.
My whiskers help me see in the dark.
I lick my paws.
What am I?

Answer: A dog.

## Henry Morriss (6)
Pitsford School, Pitsford

# Who Am I?

I take care of my friends.
I have a good memory.
I make a noise when I play.
I get lonely.
I am a chatterbox.
I have a tail.
What am I?

Answer: A rat.

## Noah Hulme (7)
Pitsford School, Pitsford

# Snap

I have a swirly tail.
I can swim.
I live on an island.
I am green.
I have lots of teeth.
What am I?

Answer: A crocodile.

## Henry Schwartz-Jones (5)
Pitsford School, Pitsford

# Pets

I have whiskers.
I play with string.
You could have me as a pet.
I like to scratch.
I miaow.
What am I?

Answer: A cat.

**Erin Amirak (6)**
Pitsford School, Pitsford

# Camouflage

I look like a shadow.
I don't roar.
I live in the jungle.
I eat meat.
I can pounce.
What am I?

Answer: A panther.

## Ava Thompson (5)
Pitsford School, Pitsford

# Fast

I have four legs.
I live in a zoo.
I might eat you.
I make people cry.
I run fast.
What am I?

Answer: A cheetah.

## Hannah Muriva (5)
Pitsford School, Pitsford

# Spotty

I can fly.
I have six legs.
I have antlers.
I eat leaves.
I make people happy.
What am I?

Answer: A ladybird.

## Isla McNally (6)
Pitsford School, Pitsford

# The Sweet Brown Thing

I'm as sweet as a bag of sugar.
I'm like a chocolate delight.
You put me in the oven for thirty minutes.
You normally have me for your pudding.
I'm as sweet as a gummy bear.
I'm as squelchy as a sponge.
What am I?

Answer: A chocolate cake.

## Leyton Considine (7)
St Luke's CE Primary School, Duston

# Chocolate Takes Over

I am spongy, gloopy, delicious, chocolatey, slurpy and sticky.
I'm as yummy as sugar.
I am as brown as mud.
I'm good for pudding
And you can buy me in Sainsbury's for birthdays and Christmas.
What am I?

Answer: A chocolate cake.

## Shanice Makoni (6)
St Luke's CE Primary School, Duston

# Grey And Heavy

I live in a desert.
I have four legs.
I eat green grass to keep me healthy.
I have a long tail and it's swishy.
I have big, floppy ears and I'm big.
I am an omnivore and I'm grey and heavy.
What am I?

Answer: An elephant.

## Rylee Star Sawyer (6)
St Luke's CE Primary School, Duston

# Cold, Drippy And Yummy Stuff

I am as cold as the snowy wintertime.
I am sweeter than a sour peppermint.
When you are hot come and get me.
I can be any flavour.
If you saw me you would want to eat me!
What flavour would you pick?
What am I?

Answer: An ice cream.

## Sienna Tomes (7)
St Luke's CE Primary School, Duston

# The Prey Chaser

I have eight legs.
I am small.
I am quite long.
I eat insects.
I have leaf-shaped, choppy claws.
I am black and I can also be red sometimes.
I hunt other prey.
I can be poisonous.
What am I?

Answer: A scorpion.

## Alice Olivia Abdy (6)
St Luke's CE Primary School, Duston

# Fluffy Fairy

I have thick, woolly skin like a blanket.
I like drinking lots of yummy milk.
I am little and cuddly.
If you touch me I might purr.
I like eating white fish so much.
I like bouncing in a house.
What am I?

Answer: A cat.

## Lily Grace Birch (6)
St Luke's CE Primary School, Duston

# Big Bird

I am fast and I am as big as a tiger.
I fly in the blue sky and I am a good hunter.
I have a yellow beak.
I live in a brown nest.
I live in the high mountains.
I love eating yummy fish.
What am I?

Answer: An eagle.

## Caleb Tew (6)
St Luke's CE Primary School, Duston

# Lovely Treat

I'm good for summer.
I'm as cold as snow.
I'm very yummy.
I'm lovely with chocolate sauce.
I go in the freezer.
Everyone loves me.
I'm a lovely treat.
What am I?

Answer: An ice cream.

## Bella Maranzano (7)
St Luke's CE Primary School, Duston

# Little Friend

I purr really loud.
I like fish.
I run fast.
I scratch people.
I hiss at people.
I have four legs.
I have black and pink ears.
I have triangular ears.
I have stripes.
What am I?

Answer: A cat.

## Sasha Chikandwa (6)
St Luke's CE Primary School, Duston

# The Furriest

I am as furry as a blanket.
I have furry ears.
I like napping in the daytime.
I have four strong legs.
I bark at night-time.
I like chewing my bones.
I love being played with.
What am I?

Answer: A dog.

**Lucy-Anne Hever (6)**
St Luke's CE Primary School, Duston

# What Am I?

I have a cone on the bottom.
I am filled with chocolate.
My flavour can be strawberry, vanilla or chocolate.
I can be found in shops.
I am often eaten at the beach.
What am I?

Answer: An ice cream.

## Lamont Tristan M (6)
St Luke's CE Primary School, Duston

# What Would You Like?

I have a cone at the bottom.
I am pointy at the end.
I can be any flavour.
You can have me when you're hot.
You have me at a party.
I am as cold as ice.
What am I?

Answer: An ice cream.

## Sophia Mabuto (7)
St Luke's CE Primary School, Duston

# Brown And Delicious

I am as yummy as an apple.
I am as chocolatey as a chocolate water slide.
I'm as messy as tomato sauce.
I'm the yummiest thing on Earth.
I am creamy.
What am I?

Answer: Chocolate cake.

## Maegan Nicole Anderton (6)
St Luke's CE Primary School, Duston

# I Am A Summer Fruit

I am as prickly as a caterpillar.
I am sweet like a lollipop.
I am green and brown like an autumn leaf.
I'm hard like a metal spoon.
I am a cool fruit.
What am I?

Answer: A kiwi fruit.

## Isla Eve Redding (7)
St Luke's CE Primary School, Duston

# Speedy

I am as spotty as a dog.
I am as speedy as a horse.
I live in the jungle.
I am as fluffy as a cat.
I am as terrifying as a tiger.
I am as big as a lion.
What am I?

Answer: A cheetah.

## Harry Timothy Roberts (5)
St Luke's CE Primary School, Duston

# Sweets And Treats

I am very chewy.
I am very delicious.
You have to get me at the shops.
There are a lot of different types of me.
I am a sweet.
I have different flavours.
What am I?

Answer: Haribos.

## Zack Linnane (7)
St Luke's CE Primary School, Duston

# Midnight Hunter

I am as furry as a blanket.
I live in the dark, dark woods.
I come out at night.
I am as orange as an orange.
I have little pointy ears.
I like autumn.
What am I?

Answer: A fox.

## Ryan Woodfield (6)
St Luke's CE Primary School, Duston

# Topping Food

I am hot.
I can be cooked in the oven.
I am yummy.
I like to be eaten for dinner.
Some of my toppings are spicy.
I have crusts filled with cheese.
What am I?

Answer: A pizza.

## Luke Try (6)
St Luke's CE Primary School, Duston

# The Lumpy Food

I'm bumpy like a rock.
I'm swirly as a worm.
What do you think I taste of?
Eat me now because I taste yummy!
I'm delicious as a crisp.
What am I?

Answer: Pasta bake.

## Evie Clark (6)
St Luke's CE Primary School, Duston

# Swirly Delight

I am as cold as ice.
Sprinkle hundreds and thousands over me.
Some like chocolate, vanilla or strawberry.
Scoop me up and put me in a crunchy cone.
What am I?

Answer: An ice cream.

## Anelise Otilia Stanciu (7)
St Luke's CE Primary School, Duston

# Long-Legged

I have four legs.
I have a small tail.
I have a tiny head.
I have lots and lots of spots.
I eat long grass.
I have the longest neck!
What am I?

Answer: A giraffe.

## Lily-Mae Richards (6)
St Luke's CE Primary School, Duston

# Big Cat

I have a long tail.
I hide in long, green grass.
I hunt for my food.
My hair is orange.
I am a big cat.
I have a furry, golden mane.
What am I?

Answer: A lion.

**Lily Sue Frost (6)**
St Luke's CE Primary School, Duston

# Stripy

I have four legs.
I live in Africa.
I have a short neck.
I eat green grass.
I am white and black.
I look like a horse but I am not.
What am I?

Answer: A zebra.

## Jessie Ivy Rose Lodge (6)
St Luke's CE Primary School, Duston

# Burning Brown Spot

I'm as brown as a biscuit.
I am some food.
I'm as round as a circle.
I am not a face.
I am not healthy, you get me at the shop.
What am I?

Answer: A cookie.

## Jenson Falkner (6)
St Luke's CE Primary School, Duston

# A Big Cat

I like to eat everything.
I am a sort of cat.
I have black stripes on me.
I am furry and soft.
I roar really loudly.
I eat meat.
What am I?

Answer: A tiger.

## Katarina Berberic (6)
St Luke's CE Primary School, Duston

# They Mess Around

I am stripy and cuddly.
I like playing in the shiny sand.
I live in the hot desert.
I love messing around.
I eat yucky scorpions.
What am I?

Answer: A meerkat.

## Amelia-Rose Richardson (5)
St Luke's CE Primary School, Duston

# Green Sea Diver

I have a hard shell.
I walk very slowly.
I munch on green plants.
I have big scales and I am green.
I dive into the blue sea.
What am I?

Answer: A sea turtle.

## Annabelle Brown (6)
St Luke's CE Primary School, Duston

# Big Cat

I have four legs.
I am covered in soft fur.
I am quite big.
I eat meat because I am a meat-eater.
I have lots of big spots.
What am I?

Answer: A cheetah.

**Daniel Rees (6)**
St Luke's CE Primary School, Duston

# I'm Light, Dark And Sweet

I melt when you point me at the sun.
I'm light and dark.
I'm red and black.
I cannot run.
I cannot talk.
What am I?

*Answer: Strawberry chocolate.*

## Joy Bonsu (7)
St Luke's CE Primary School, Duston

# What Is It?

It is my favourite food in Great Yarmouth on holiday.
It is red and sweet.
It is tasty to eat.
It is red and brown.
What am I?

Answer: A chocolate strawberry.

## Alice Shepherd (7)
St Luke's CE Primary School, Duston

# Hunter

I have four, hairy legs.
I am as fast as a car.
I am spotty.
I have got whiskers.
I like meat.
I am yellow and black.
What am I?

Answer: A cheetah.

## Archie Ronald Britten (6)
St Luke's CE Primary School, Duston

# The Yummy Brown Slice

Beware as I'm as delicate as china.
I'm as brown as mud.
I'm a brown triangle.
I'm as tasty as chocolate.
What am I?

Answer: A piece of cake.

## Harrison Lovekin (7)
St Luke's CE Primary School, Duston

# The Little Cutie

I am as soft as a blanket.
I can purr and purr.
I have a pattern.
I have big, bright eyes.
I have long, black whiskers.
What am I?

Answer: A cat.

## Fleur Boobyer (5)
St Luke's CE Primary School, Duston

# Fluffy Animals

I have a woolly, fluffy coat.
I like to chew a bone.
I have four strong legs.
I am always happy.
I like chasing balls.
What am I?

Answer: A dog.

## Grace Lauren Louise Dolman (6)
St Luke's CE Primary School, Duston

# I Don't Like Water

I am as furry as a blanket.
I like milk.
I don't like water.
I like lying in the sun.
I purr when you stroke me.
What am I?

Answer: A cat.

## Paige Hayward (5)
St Luke's CE Primary School, Duston

# Yummy Yummy

I am delicious and scrumptious.
I am yummy and nice.
I have cheese and sauce on.
I have pepperoni.
People love me.
What am I?

Answer: A pizza.

## Charlie Littlewood (6)
St Luke's CE Primary School, Duston

# Spiky Thing

Don't touch me, I am spiky.
I am wet like a puddle.
My colour is apple-green.
Sometimes I burn your red tongue.
What am I?

Answer: A pineapple.

**Lewis Smith (6)**
St Luke's CE Primary School, Duston

# Fast Jumper

I am fluffy like a cloud.
I have soft, brown fur.
I am as small as a cat.
I love to jump high.
I have long ears.
What am I?

Answer: A rabbit.

## Abbie Renda (6)
St Luke's CE Primary School, Duston

# Sweet Yummy Stuff

I am like a bag of sugar.
I taste like something yellow.
I am a whole piece.
You can eat me at a birthday party!
What am I?

Answer: A cheesecake.

## Paige McDonnell (6)
St Luke's CE Primary School, Duston

# I Am Fast

I am the fastest animal.
I am fluffy and cosy.
I live in the jungle.
I have sharp claws.
I am a wild animal.
What am I?

*Answer: A cheetah.*

## Rishab Jain (5)
St Luke's CE Primary School, Duston

# Delicious Roundness

I am round and brown.
You can cut me into slices.
You can put strawberries on top of me
And lots of cream.
What am I?

Answer: A chocolate cake.

**Tony Singh (6)**
St Luke's CE Primary School, Duston

# Dark Night

I'm as dark as a blackbird.
I'm as rectangular as a car.
You will like me if you eat me.
Eat me now!
What am I?

*Answer: Dark chocolate.*

## Lewis Pearson (6)
St Luke's CE Primary School, Duston

# Amazing Italy

I am bows that you don't put in your hair.
I am covered in delicious tomato sauce
And with yellow cheese on top.
What am I?

Answer: Pasta bows.

## Iulia Duta (6)
St Luke's CE Primary School, Duston

# Tremendous Triangles

I am cheesy.
I am shaped like a triangle.
You pick me up with your fingers,
Then lick your yummy fingers.
What am I?

Answer: Cheesy nachos.

## Zachary Morley (6)
St Luke's CE Primary School, Duston

# Big Animal

I have four legs.
I am massive.
I am grey.
I have long ears.
I like peanuts.
I have a long trunk.
What am I?

Answer: An elephant.

## Andrei Marinescu (6)
St Luke's CE Primary School, Duston

# Soft

I am really fluffy.
I can have dark or light fur.
I jump high!
I have four legs.
I love orange carrots.
What am I?

Answer: A rabbit.

## Jessica Redzaj (5)
St Luke's CE Primary School, Duston

# A Big Cat

I eat meat.
You cannot see me in the grass.
I have sharp teeth.
I am a type of cat.
I run really fast.
What am I?

Answer: A cheetah.

## Arthur Haslam (5)
St Luke's CE Primary School, Duston

# Fish Lover!

I have four legs.
I have soft fur.
My fur is dark.
I eat fish.
I can roar loudly!
I live in a cave.
What am I?

Answer: A bear.

## Callum Muldoon (5)
St Luke's CE Primary School, Duston

# The Green

I can eat you and suck you up.
I live in America.
I live in water.
I have sharp teeth.
I am fierce.
What am I?

Answer: A crocodile.

## Ashden Copeland (5)
St Luke's CE Primary School, Duston

# Delicious

I am delicious.
I am as brown as an old coin.
I'm so nice.
What a good snack I am.
I am yummy.
What am I?

Answer: A burger.

## Emily Cripps (6)
St Luke's CE Primary School, Duston

# Colourful Food

I'm as colourful as a rainbow.
I'm as long as a giraffe's neck.
I'm as yummy as an ice cream.
What am I?

Answer: Sushi.

## Maksymilian Wojciechowski (7)
St Luke's CE Primary School, Duston

# Fluffy

I have sharp claws.
I have a fluffy body.
I have dirty feet.
I like to play outside.
I bark a lot.
What am I?

Answer: A dog.

## Noah Hyliands (5)
St Luke's CE Primary School, Duston

# Sea Diver

I eat green, green grass.
I am green all over.
I dive in the deep blue sea.
I have a hard shell.
What am I?

Answer: A sea turtle.

## Micah Siziba (5)
St Luke's CE Primary School, Duston

# Very Spicy

I am as spicy as a chilli.
I am small.
I am a triangular shape.
I am as soft as white bread.
What am I?

Answer: A slice of pizza.

## Sebastian Jeffreys (7)
St Luke's CE Primary School, Duston

# Crunchy Food

I am lots of different flavours.
I'm as crunchy as an ice cream cone.
What a good piece of food I am!
What am I?

Answer: Crisps.

## Lewis Liu (7)
St Luke's CE Primary School, Duston

# Swimming Creature

I am as big as a car.
I like going in the water.
I am as hard as a table.
I like eating fish.
What am I?

Answer: A hippo.

## Elizabeth Cook (5)
St Luke's CE Primary School, Duston

# Ice Cream In A Freezer

I am cold like a freezer.
Your mouth will get cold when you eat me.
You will want me every day.
What am I?

Answer: Ice cream.

## Maisie Turner (7)
St Luke's CE Primary School, Duston

# A Small Animal

I have fur all around.
I hunt for food.
I go in your bins.
I am orange with a swishy tail.
What am I?

Answer: A fox.

## Ella May Vine (6)
St Luke's CE Primary School, Duston

# Cheesy Mess

I am hot and cheesy.
You can bite me.
I am like a triangle.
I can be bought or ordered.
What am I?

Answer: A pizza.

## Sam Connolly-Green (6)
St Luke's CE Primary School, Duston

# Crunchy Food

I'm as crunchy as an ice cube.
I'm as yummy as an ice cream.
What a good snack I am!
What am I?

Answer: Crisps.

## Krystian Redel (7)
St Luke's CE Primary School, Duston

# The Green Drumstick

I'm as green as fresh mint.
I'm as long as a drumstick.
What a good snack I am!
What am I?

Answer: A cucumber.

## Logan Hayes (7)
St Luke's CE Primary School, Duston

# Sleepy

I am furry.
I am sleepy.
I am not sleepy at night.
I like drinking milk.
I miaow.
What am I?

Answer: A cat.

## Aaron Baker (5)
St Luke's CE Primary School, Duston

# Big Bird

I am a bird.
I have two flippers.
I have a beak.
I walk slowly.
I cannot fly.
What am I?

Answer: A penguin.

## Liliko Dhesi (6)
St Luke's CE Primary School, Duston

# Fur Ball

I am soft like a softie.
I have got blue eyes.
I am orange.
I have got pointy ears.
What am I?

Answer: A cat.

## Summer Jade Anderton (5)
St Luke's CE Primary School, Duston

# I Am Yummy Food

I am colourful like a rainbow.
I am shaped like a circle or square.
I am a yummy snack.
What am I?

Answer: A cake.

## Ameena Abimbola Adekoya (7)

St Luke's CE Primary School, Duston

# Sea Creature

I am small.
I have a shell.
I live in water.
I have four legs.
I am green.
What am I?

Answer: A turtle.

## Elliot King (5)
St Luke's CE Primary School, Duston

# Spotty Cat

You cannot ride on me.
I have soft fur.
I can run really fast.
I am a big cat.
What am I?

Answer: A cheetah.

## Ava-Mae Lowry (5)
St Luke's CE Primary School, Duston

# Happy And Chunky

I have a tail.
I have a shiny coat.
I like to play in the mud.
I run really fast.
What am I?

Answer: A dog.

## Grayson Hughes (5)
St Luke's CE Primary School, Duston

# Fast Cat

I have four legs.
I am fast at running.
I hunt for my food.
I am very spotty.
What am I?

Answer: A cheetah.

## Zakaria Kunhalil (6)
St Luke's CE Primary School, Duston

# A Lot Of Sweetness

I am fruity.
I am juicy.
I am chewy.
I am found in shops.
I have wrappers.
What am I?

Answer: Sweets.

## Imogen Castle (6)
St Luke's CE Primary School, Duston

# Fast Animal

I am as fast as a car.
I am spotty.
I have four legs.
I am yellow and black.
What am I?

Answer: A cheetah.

## Oscar Gibbins (6)
St Luke's CE Primary School, Duston

# Whiskers

I have white whiskers.
I love to stretch.
I say *miaow*!
I love my food.
What am I?

Answer: A cat.

**Aurelia Taylor (4)**
St Luke's CE Primary School, Duston

# Prickly Friend

I have four legs.
I have leaves and insects for tea.
I have a big, brown back.
What am I?

Answer: A hedgehog.

## Ruben Holt (6)
St Luke's CE Primary School, Duston

# What Am I?

I fly in the sky.
I have warm feathers.
I live in a tree.
I am colourful.
What am I?

Answer: A toucan.

## Scarlett Lily-May Craven (5)
St Luke's CE Primary School, Duston

# Leaf Lover

I have four legs.
I can walk and run.
I have a long neck to eat green leaves.
What am I?

Answer: A giraffe.

## Harley Nichols (6)
St Luke's CE Primary School, Duston

# Chewy Thing

I am chewy like meat.
I get stuck between your teeth.
I look like a circle.
What am I?

Answer: A steak.

## Leo V (6)
St Luke's CE Primary School, Duston

# Swinger Animal

I am covered in hair.
I live in the forest.
I swing through the trees.
What am I?

Answer: A chimpanzee.

## George Hamer (5)
St Luke's CE Primary School, Duston

# Fluffy

I am fluffy.
I have four legs.
I like sleeping.
I say *miaow*.
What am I?

Answer: A cat.

## Vinnie Ogden (5)
St Luke's CE Primary School, Duston

# Magical Food

I taste good.
I am a good snack.
I am delicious.
I am yellow.
What am I?

Answer: French fries.

## Filip Chomicki (6)
St Luke's CE Primary School, Duston

# Cheeky

I am fluffy.
I eat bananas.
I swing in the trees.
I drink a lot.
What am I?

Answer: A monkey.

## Poppy Kenton (5)
St Luke's CE Primary School, Duston

# Fresh And Cold

I am as cold as snow.
Kids love me.
You can eat me on the beach.
What am I?

Answer: An ice cream.

**Noah Morris (7)**
St Luke's CE Primary School, Duston

# What Food Am I?

I am very tasty and meaty.
I'm so good.
Sometimes I get cooked.
What am I?

Answer: Chicken.

## Faith Brothers (7)

St Luke's CE Primary School, Duston

# What Am I?

I live in the house.
I have fur.
I go *woof*.
What am I?

Answer: A dog.

## Erioluwa Tioluwa Nathan Oyetunde (5)

St Luke's CE Primary School, Duston

# What Am I?

I like milk.
I like fish.
I go *miaow*.
What am I?

Answer: A cat.

## Isioma Divine Ohaeli (4)

St Luke's CE Primary School, Duston

# What Am I?

I am a fruit, I live on a tree indeed
I have many friends, in the middle I have a
seed
My friends are like me
In my beautiful green tree
You can find me in a pie.
What am I?

Answer: A cherry.

## Julia Wozniak (6)
Upton Meadows Primary School, Upton

Young**Writers**
Est.1991

# YOUNG WRITERS
# INFORMATION

We hope you have enjoyed reading this book – and that you will continue to in the coming years.

If you're a young writer who enjoys reading and creative writing, or the parent of an enthusiastic poet or story writer, do visit our website **www.youngwriters.co.uk**. Here you will find free competitions, workshops and games, as well as recommended reads, a poetry glossary and our blog.

If you would like to order further copies of this book, or any of our other titles, then please give us a call or visit **www.youngwriters.co.uk**.

Young Writers
Remus House
Coltsfoot Drive
Peterborough
PE2 9BF
(01733) 890066
info@youngwriters.co.uk